Life Skills Every
8 YEAR OLD
Should Know

Unlock Your Secret Superpowers
and Succeed in All Areas of Life

HAYDEN FOX

CLAIM YOUR FREE GIFTS!

(My way of saying thank you for your support)

Simply visit
haydenfoxmedia.com
to receive the following:

10 Powerful Dinner Conversations
To Create Amazing Kids

10 Magnificent Affirmations
To Help Kids Become Unstoppable In Life

SCAN ME

(You can also scan this QR code)

This book belongs to

_____

● TABLE OF CONTENTS ●

INTRODUCTION

Hey, kids! Eight years old is such a tough place to be. You're getting bigger and wiser, but you still feel like there's so much more to learn. As you grow, there's more to learn than just what you hear in school. You're on your way to becoming a grown-up, and that's pretty cool!

But, it can be pretty scary too! Grown-ups have some big jobs to do. Think about the grown-ups in your life that take care of you. Maybe it's Mom and Dad. Maybe it's Grandma, Uncle, or someone else. What do they do for you?

They cook, right? And clean? They take care of you? They bring you to school and help with homework? They help you get over fights? That seems like a whole lot of stuff, and you might think there's no way you could do ALL those things!

And you're right. Some of those things you can't do yet. But, you can start learning the steps. You can start learning how to cook, how to get along with friends and brothers and sisters, and lots of other things, too.

That's what this book is here for. This book is a guide of thirteen skills that every eight-year-old should start learning. They might seem hard at first, but if you break them down into little steps and ask for help when you need it, you'll learn they're not so bad.

Before we start talking about the things you need to know, there's one important thing to start with. If you start trying to learn some of these skills and they're too hard or you don't get it right, that's okay! You're still learning. Every grown-up had to learn these things too, and it wasn't always easy.

If you're stuck on something, ask your trusted grown-up for help. Ask them if there was a time they had a hard time doing what you're trying to do. Remember, your grown-up was a kid once too! They might have some stories that will help you feel better when things are hard for you.

It's not always easy to learn a new thing. Was it easy to learn how to read and write? Or how to do math? No! But did you give up? If you're reading this book, then you kept trying and you learned how to read! It took time, and it took practice, but you did it.

Think about video games. When you start playing a new game, how strong is your character? Probably not very! You start out at level 1, where you start learning how to play, right? These skills are just like that. You start out at level 1, and you practice and practice until you level up. If you give up, then you never level up, and you never learn.

You aren't failing until you stop trying, so even when things are hard, remember that!

As you read, you'll start learning all sorts of new things that will help you now and as you grow up. You'll learn about how to break down hard tasks, how to set goals that will help you succeed, and you'll learn a lot of other things too. Once you learn them, they'll get easier and easier with practice. One day, you'll be surprised at how hard it seemed the first time you tried.

Are you ready to start learning new things? Let's get reading!

Chapter 1

HOW TO MAKE A HARD DECISION

Has there ever been a time where you had to make a decision that seemed impossible? Maybe you had to choose whether you wanted chocolate ice cream with sprinkles or vanilla ice cream with a cherry. Maybe it was a harder choice, like a friend asking you to do something that you know is against the rules.

Making hard choices can be tough, especially when you know that choosing to do something will be fun, even if it's something you're not supposed to do. Even grown-ups face hard choices sometimes. In the section below, you will find some easy tricks that will help you the next time you find yourself between a rock and a hard place.

CONSEQUENCES AND YOUR DECISIONS

Do you know what a consequence is?

A **consequence** is the result of something that you do. It can be good or bad. A good consequence could be making your friends happy by giving them a gift. A bad consequence could be a time-out after breaking a rule.

Every decision you make has good and bad consequences. Thinking about those consequences can help you make the right decision.

Let's say you really want to stay up late on a school night. Maybe you're reading a book that you just can't put down, so you hide under your blanket to read it all night long. The next morning, when it's time to wake up, you're still really sleepy. You're sleepy all day long at school. You're sleepy all afternoon, and you're sleepy all evening.

Was staying up late worth the consequence?

When you think about consequences before you make a decision, you can decide if those consequences are worth making that choice. If you don't do your homework, you might not get to go to recess at school, or play video games after school. If you don't clean your room, your parents may take away privileges like playing with friends or take the toys you left on the floor.

The next time you're making a decision to do or not do something, stop and think about what will happen next.

THE RIGHT THING AND THE FUN THING

Sometimes, decisions can be between doing the right thing and the fun thing. The fun thing might be breaking a rule, like sneaking ice cream before dinner, or playing a prank on a brother or sister. Sometimes, the fun thing isn't the right thing at all. Is it right for someone to hide a spider in their sister's room because they think her screaming in horror is funny? No!

What about making a promise to go to a friend's house, and then another friend invites you to go to a movie? Is it nice to go watch the movie because it sounds like more fun when you already promised someone else you'd do something together? That's another hard decision to make, but it's important to follow through when you say you will do something, even if it's not fun.

MAKING PROS AND CONS LISTS

I know, I know. Writing lists sounds like one of the most boring ways in the world to make a decision. It's also a really good way to look at the pros and cons of a decision before you make it. Your list of pros will be a list of all the good things you can think of happening if you do something. Your list of cons will be a list of all the bad things you can think of happening if you do something.

Maybe you are weighing the pros and cons of whether to sneak a piece of candy when you're in bed after you already brushed your teeth. Your list might look something like this:

Pros:

- I get to eat a yummy piece of candy.

- It will make me happy to eat it.

Cons:

- Mom and Dad will be upset.

- I will feel bad for breaking the rules.

- I might get in trouble.

- Eating candy and sleeping is bad for my teeth.

Looking at that list, does it seem like sneaking a piece of candy before bed is a good thing or a bad thing? To me, it looks like there are more cons than pros, so it would be a bad decision.

ASKING FOR HELP

When you're stuck on a really hard decision, don't forget to ask for help if you need it. Sometimes, talking to a grown-up, an older sibling, a teacher, or a trusted friend can help you better make a decision because you get more perspectives. Perspectives are other people's ways of seeing the world around us, and sometimes, other people can see things we might not.

TAKING RESPONSIBILITY WHEN YOU MAKE A BAD DECISION

Uh oh! Did you make a bad decision? Maybe you decided not to feed your dog because you were too busy playing, and they were hungry all morning. Maybe you decided to throw a rock and it broke a window.

When you make a decision, it's important to take responsibility for it. This means taking **accountability** for your decision. Accountability is when you admit that something that happened was your fault, and if it was a bad thing, you do something to make it right.

This means you may owe someone an apology, but you will feel better after you do!

Chapter 2

HOW TO SET GOALS SO YOU CAN ACHIEVE THEM

Have you ever decided that you wanted to do something, but then gave up on it because it seemed too hard? Everyone has done it before, even the grown-ups in your life. Maybe you wanted to write a whole story on your own, or you wanted to finish a project early.

Have you ever noticed that when you build a playset with blocks, it's easier to follow the directions than it is to try to make a whole building on your own? That's because the instructions act as a map you can use to finish the project. What if you had a way that you could do this on your own?

Setting goals the right way is like making a map that will guide you to the finish line. Learning how to set a goal isn't hard, either. All you have to do is remember SMART!

SMART GOALS

SMART goals are goals that are:

- **S**pecific
- **M**easurable
- **A**ttainable
- **R**elevant
- **T**imely

If you work your way down the list when setting your goal, you end up with a plan that tells you exactly how to achieve it.

Let's say you have a goal to get better at playing soccer and set a SMART goal to help. You can also follow along with your own goal and write it down in a notebook so you can start working on it.

SPECIFIC

Goals have to be specific so you know what you are trying to do. Getting better at playing soccer isn't a very specific goal. Instead of saying you want to get better, choose something more specific. Maybe you decide to say your goal is to dribble a soccer ball without messing up. That's a much more specific goal and gives you a clear idea of what achieving it will look like.

MEASURABLE

Goals have to be measurable so we can track our progress as we work toward them. Think of this like reaching checkpoints in a video game level. At every checkpoint, you're one step closer to finishing the level.

Maybe your goal is that you want to dribble a soccer ball all the way across the soccer field without messing up. You know you've achieved your goal when you can see that you made it from one side of the field to the next.

ACHIEVABLE

Goals need to be something that you can actually achieve, even if it will be difficult to do it. Is it possible for you to dribble a soccer ball all the way across the field? Maybe not if you have a broken leg. If you broke your leg, this would not be an achievable goal because you wouldn't be able to run across the field.

RELEVANT

When something is relevant, it's something that matters. A goal should be relevant to you, meaning it's something you really care about or need to do. Does it make sense for you to decide to dribble a soccer ball across a field? It might not matter to someone who plays baseball or does gymnastics, but if you play soccer, then it would be relevant to you.

TIME-BOUND

When something is time-bound, it's like having a due date or deadline for it. We want our goals to have a deadline so we are held accountable and feel like it's important to meet it.

Maybe you decide that by the end of summer, you want to be able to dribble a soccer ball all the way across the soccer field. This means you have to practice all summer so you can reach your goal.

WORKING TOWARD SMART GOALS

Working toward SMART goals might seem scary at first, but you can do it! I like to set mini checkpoints in my goals to help me keep some progress. So, if you wanted to work toward a goal of dribbling the soccer ball across the field by the end of summer, you might say that you want to be able to dribble the ball ¼ the way down the field by the end of June, ¾ the way down the field by the end of July, and all the way to the end by the end of summer.

The more you work toward your goals and the more you achieve them, the better you will feel about yourself. It can really build a lot of confidence as you see how capable you are.

Don't forget, if you feel stuck when trying to set up a goal, it's always okay to ask for help!

Chapter 3

HOW TO SAY NO

Has someone ever asked you to do something that made you *really* uncomfortable? Maybe a classmate tried to get you to break a rule. Or maybe your sibling wanted you to help them sneak something or keep a secret.

It can be hard to tell someone no when they are a friend or someone you like, or if everyone else is doing the thing that you don't want to do. Some kids will do it just because they want to fit in, or because they don't want to be made fun of. However, this isn't good for you.

If someone is trying to make you do something that makes you uncomfortable, it's important to stand up for yourself, and ask for help from a grown-up if you need it.

BEING ASSERTIVE

Being assertive means you are being firm in your decision. Does your grown-up ever look at you and firmly tell you that you can't do something? This means your grown-up is being assertive.

It can be hard to be assertive if it's not something you've done before. Being assertive will help you to stand up for yourself and your beliefs so you don't feel pressured to do something you don't want to do. Learning to be assertive helps you communicate how you feel in a way that is calm so you can keep your control over yourself and the situation.

To be assertive, you need to share your feelings in a firm, but still respectful, way. For example, you might calmly say,

"No, I don't want to do that because I feel like it's wrong and I don't want to get in trouble."

It helps to make eye contact with the other person while talking to them so you know they are listening.

A mistake a lot of kids and grown-ups make is being aggressive instead of assertive when standing up for themselves. This means maybe deciding to yell, be bossy, argue, or call someone names. Aggression happens when you lose control of your anger.

WHEN YOU SHOULD SAY NO

Have you ever heard of peer pressure? It's when your peers, or people your age, try to get you to do something or act a certain way, making you feel like you have to do it to fit in.

Sometimes, the things that your peers do or say are things that you feel are wrong or bad. They might want you to break a rule, or to act in a way that makes you uncomfortable, like saying you need to help them make fun of another kid at school.

Whenever something makes you feel uncomfortable, or it's something that you know is against the rules, you should say no. It's also a good idea to tell a trusted grown-up, like a parent or a teacher, if your peers are pressuring you.

COMPROMISING INSTEAD OF SAYING NO

Sometimes, you might not want to do something that someone else is asking you to do right that minute. It could be that a friend or family member wants to play with you, but you're happy reading your book or drawing a picture.

It can sometimes help you to say, "Not right now," instead of "No," to someone if it's something that you think you might want to do another time.

For example, if your friend asks you to play tag, you could tell your friend, "No, I don't want to do that right now, but I will play tag with you after I finish drawing this picture."

This is a sort of compromise that helps you to do what you want while still feeling like you aren't letting the other person down.

Chapter 4

HOW TO SOLVE A PROBLEM

Everyone faces problems. They can be small problems, like accidentally spilling milk, or big problems, like not knowing what to do after you get into a fight with a friend, or accidentally breaking something important. Maybe your problem is that the cool project you're working on just isn't working out.

When you look at problems as the chance to experiment with something, it can be a lot easier to work through it. In science class, you probably learned about thinking like a scientist. You make a hypothesis (an informed guess), and then you test it.

Problem-solving is a lot like this. You identify a problem and make a hypothesis on how to solve it. Then, you choose which of your possible solutions is the most likely to work and test it. If it works, then great! You solved your problem! If it doesn't work, then you just go back and try another possible solution.

IDENTIFYING THE PROBLEM

Sometimes, saying your problem out loud can help you feel a lot better. It's scary when you face a problem you don't know how to solve, but saying it out loud can help you start thinking about how to fix it.

Maybe you say, "None of my friends want to play tag with me during recess." This helps you because you are expressing how you feel while also identifying the problem. That's the first step to getting unstuck.

COMING UP WITH POSSIBLE SOLUTIONS

If you have a problem that needs to be solved, it's good to come up with lots of solutions. Try to come up with at least five when you face a big problem. Sometimes, you might only come up with two or three and that's okay!

It doesn't matter what the solutions you come up with are right now, as long as you think that they could solve the problem. For example, if your problem is that your friends won't play with you, maybe you come up with a list that looks like this:

1. I could try asking someone new to play with me.

2. I could try asking my friends to play a different game with me.

3. I could try playing the game my friends are playing.

4. I could try to have fun climbing on the playground by myself.

5. I could try joining a game with other kids instead of my friends.

All of these are different things you could try to do to have fun at recess. The next step is trying to choose which one to start with.

MAKING A PROS AND CONS LIST

To decide which solution to try, come up with the pros and cons for each one, just like you did when trying to make a big decision. Let's start with the first solution, asking someone new to play with you.

Pros

- I could make new friends.

- I could have fun playing during recess.

- I could learn a new game.

Cons

- They might say no and I could be embarrassed.

- I might not like them when we start playing.

CHOOSE A SOLUTION FROM YOUR LIST

Once you make your list of pros and cons, you can choose the one that has the most pros and give it a shot. Maybe you decide that trying to play the game your friends are playing is the best choice after looking at the pros and cons of all your options.

TEST THE SOLUTION

Now, you try it! Go up to your friends and ask if you can play kickball with them. They might say yes, and you will have a great time with them. Or, they might say no.

REPEAT!

If your solution fails, all you have to do is choose another one from your list and try again. It's time to put your scientist jacket on and keep on trying until you find the right fix!

Don't feel bad if your first solution doesn't work! In life, our first attempts at fixing a problem often don't work out how we plan them. That's okay! It's okay to feel disappointed if your solution doesn't work, but remember, you only fail if you stop trying.

If you really get stuck, don't forget that it's always okay to go to a trusted grown-up for help. You can talk about the problem with them and learn some new ways to try to solve it.

Chapter 5

HOW TO HANDLE BIG EMOTIONS

Do you ever feel so angry it feels like you can't control yourself? What about being so sad that you don't want to do anything at all? Have you ever been so frustrated with something that you give up instead of trying again?

Everyone has big emotions sometimes. Yes, even grown-ups! We all get mad or sad or frustrated or disappointed, and that's okay. Feelings happen to everyone, and we can't really control them, but just because we can't control them doesn't mean we have to let them control us.

Learning how to handle big emotions can help you make better decisions. You can learn to not throw your toy in anger or give up in frustration by learning to express your feelings in a healthy way.

One thing to remember is that feeling big emotions isn't a bad thing. When you feel very strongly about something, it's a way for you to learn more about yourself and how you react. It's also a way for you to grow stronger because you are learning important lessons about yourself and other people.

TAKE DEEP BREATHS

When you feel a strong emotion that is making it hard to control yourself, a good idea to help calm yourself down is called grounding. No, not like the kind when you get in trouble. This kind of grounding is kind of like a plant sinking its roots into the dirt. It's finding a way to make yourself feel more stable and in control again.

One of the best ways to ground yourself is by taking deep breaths. They can't be just any breaths, though. They have to be big, deep breaths.

To do this, all you have to do is breathe in through your nose while you count to four. Hold your breath in your lungs and count to four again. Then, blow the air out slowly, counting to four again. Hold your breath while you count to four again. This is called square breathing.

It can take a little practice, but all you have to do is focus on your breaths while you count. Give it a try a few times now, and the next time you're feeling upset, try it then, too!

LEARN TO RECOGNIZE YOUR FEELINGS

You've probably felt so angry that your whole body felt tight and you wanted to break something or yell. You've also probably been so sad that you cried and couldn't stop. When you feel those strong feelings, it's hard to think clearly and understand why you feel that way.

It's important to know how to recognize what you are feeling so you know what to do before your feelings get too strong. This means learning to recognize how you feel and what your body does when you have strong emotions.

We all feel anger, sadness, happiness, fear, and surprise. Your body probably does some of these things when you feel them strongly.

Anger

- Flushed face

- Baring teeth

- Clenching fists

- Feeling tense

- Leaning forward at what makes you angry

- Feeling like your heart is pounding

Sadness

- Feeling droopy or melty, like you could fall down

- Crying

- Shaking lip

Happiness

- Feeling relaxed

- Smiling

- Laughing

Fear

- Feeling a cold sweat

- Shaky voice

- Crossing arms

- Feeling tense and jerky

- Shaking lips

- Not wanting to make eye contact

- Mouth feels dry

Surprise

- Wide eyes

- Raised eyebrows

- Wide open mouth

- Moving backwards

Learn these signs and when you notice that you are starting to feel strongly, stop and think about what your body is doing. If you are feeling sad, angry, or scared, knowing what you feel will help you figure out *why* you feel that way.

LEARN TO IDENTIFY WHY YOU FEEL THE WAY YOU DO

Once you know what you are feeling, it is easier to start understanding why you feel a certain way. Emotions are usually caused by something around us. They're our body's instincts or gut reactions to whatever is happening.

When you want to figure out why you feel the way you do, you can start asking yourself some questions, like:

- What happened before the strong feeling?

- What were you doing?

- What were people around you doing or saying?

- Did something unexpected happen?

- Did something you didn't like happen?

- How was your body feeling? Were you hungry? Tired? Feeling sick?

Think about the answers to your questions to figure out why you had such a strong feeling.

Imagine that you realize that you are feeling angry. Your body feels tight and tense, your fists are clenched, and your heart is racing. When you notice how you feel, you stop and take your deep breaths to calm yourself down. Then once you relax, you stop and think about it.

Maybe your brother or sister snuck into your room and accidentally broke that cool Lego project you've been working on while you were taking a bath. It was very unexpected, and you were also feeling really tired when it happened.

When your body isn't feeling its best, like when you're tired, hungry, sick, or hurt, you might get angry or upset faster. Maybe that's what happened. You would have been angry about the Lego project breaking anyway, but when you stopped and thought about it, you think that the other feelings made you feel even more angry than you should have.

CHOOSE A HEALTHY EMOTIONAL OUTLET

When we have big emotions, we usually want to let them out. Some people choose to play sports. Others play video games. Writing, reading, playing, going on walks, and even talking to friends can help you release all of your emotions.

It's important to release strong emotions instead of bottling them up. Have you ever seen what happens when someone opens a bottle of soda that's been shaken up? It explodes and makes a giant mess!

Your big emotions do the same thing when you try to push them away. Instead of letting them build up until you can't take it anymore, letting them out a little bit at a time in healthy ways keeps you from exploding. Take a look at some fun ways to let go of your strong emotions:

- Talk to someone you trust. This could be a friend or a trusted grown-up.

- Move your body! Dance to your favorite music. Go run outside with your dog or play a physical game.

- Find a creative outlet. Drawing, writing, singing, playing an instrument, or coloring are all ways you could let some emotions out.

- Take time to relax. Use your deep breathing. Take a warm bath. Count the things you see around you to calm down.

TAKE A BREAK WHEN YOU NEED ONE

Remember that it's okay to take a break if you need one. If you're feeling too overwhelmed by your emotions, it's okay to walk away for a little bit, as long as you do face them when you're feeling calmer.

The next time you get into an argument with someone and feel angry, try telling them you need a break, and take it. Sometimes, ten minutes of quiet is enough for you to feel calm enough to talk about a problem without yelling or acting out of anger.

Chapter 6

HOW TO SOLVE
A CONFLICT

Conflict can be really scary when you're in it. Maybe it's a disagreement with a friend or a sibling, or maybe you and your grown-ups don't see eye to eye. No matter what the reason for a conflict, knowing how to solve it can stop anger and frustration from growing.

Arguments and conflicts happen. Even people who like or love each other don't agree on everything, and that's okay! That's part of what makes us all different, and our differences are good. Wouldn't it be boring if we all liked and disliked the same things?

When a conflict happens, it's really easy to get upset or angry about it, and that can make the whole situation worse. Knowing how to work through a conflict with someone is one of the most important things you can learn how to do, but it also means you have to know how to deal with the big emotions we talked about in the last chapter.

WHAT NOT TO DO WHEN IN A CONFLICT

When you get into an argument with someone, there are some things you should NEVER do. These things will only make you and the other person angrier and that isn't going to help either of you solve the conflict. The next time you argue with someone, make sure you don't do these things:

- Don't call them names or use insults. This means not calling them or their ideas stupid.

- Don't hit or throw anything. You should never use violence to solve a problem.

- Don't interrupt the other person when they are talking. You and the other person should take turns talking through things so you both feel heard. The other person's feelings are just as real as yours!

- Don't refuse to listen to what the other person has to say. It's okay if you need a short break, but don't avoid the conversation forever just because you don't like what the other person has to say.

SOLVING A CONFLICT IN FIVE EASY STEPS

When you are stuck in a conflict, there are five steps that can help both you and the other person feel better so you can find a resolution. You can remember the five steps as Stop, Say, Think, Choose, and Respect.

STOP

When you notice that you and the other person aren't finding anything you can agree on, and you start arguing more, it's a good time to **stop**. Take a quick break and come together to talk about the problem after a few minutes.

SAY

Before you start trying to solve the conflict, you should **say** what you think the problem is about. Then, let the other person say what they think the problem is. You might be surprised to learn that the other person thinks the problem is something else entirely.

Maybe you think that the argument is about your little brother or sister not respecting your space because they keep going in your room. Maybe your sibling thinks that the conflict is about you not wanting to spend time with them anymore.

THINK

Once you both see what the other thinks about the conflict, or when you both agree on what the problem is, you can start **thinking** of ways to solve it. Remember the step in problem-solving, where you start thinking of solutions? Well, it's time to put those skills to good use again! Talk about ways that you and the other person could solve the problem.

Maybe you say that you'll spend more time playing with your sibling if they respect your space when you want to be alone. Is that fair? Does that meet both of your needs?

The possible solutions should be something that you both can agree on.

CHOOSE

Once you have a list of solutions, it's time to **choose** one that works for both of you. You might not both get exactly what you want, but when you both get some of what you want, you are *compromising*. Compromising means that you both settle on something that is good enough.

Maybe you and your sibling agree to a solution where if your bedroom door is shut, they stay out of it, and when it is open, it's okay for them to come in and spend time with you.

RESPECT

Sometimes, you and the other person just can't agree to something, no matter how hard you both try. When this happens, it's important to **respect** what they think and how they feel. You wouldn't like it if someone told you that your feelings were wrong, so you shouldn't do that to someone else, either.

Respect the other person's opinions, and if you can't agree on a solution, then all you can really do is agree to disagree. If it's clear that you can't agree on something together, you will just waste time arguing over and over about the same thing. This can be hurtful, frustrating, and make the whole situation worse.

Chapter 7

HOW TO MAKE FRIENDS

Do you have lots of friends, or do you have just one or two? Different people will make friends in different ways. That's just one of those things that makes us unique. Some people are happier with just a few close friends, while others prefer to have lots of different friends to talk to and play with.

Sometimes, people find themselves in situations where they have to make new friends. If you've ever moved to a new neighborhood or school before, you probably had to start meeting new friends. This can be super scary sometimes, but there are some easy ways that you can make friends without having to be afraid.

WHY MAKING FRIENDS CAN BE HARD

Some kids have a hard time making friends for all sorts of reasons. If making friends is hard for you, it might be because of one of these reasons:

You're afraid other people won't like you or you'll be embarrassed if you try to make friends with them.

- You can't find things that you have in common with the people around you.

- You're hard on yourself and always compare yourself to other people. Maybe you see a classmate who seems to make friends with everyone and think that you're not as good or smart or funny as that other person.

- You're shy or nervous about meeting new people.

- You don't know what to say when you meet new people.

TIPS FOR MAKING NEW FRIENDS

If you feel like some of the points listed above describe you, then you might need some help learning how to make friends. Even if some people seem to know how to make friends naturally, it is something that needs to be learned for many. It's okay if you feel like it's harder for you than it is for other kids your age. If it really bothers you, then you can start practicing making friends and meeting new people. Remember, everything gets easier the more you practice it!

FIND COMMON GROUND

Common ground is another way to say that you and someone else have something in common. Think about friends you've had in the past. Are they people who have the same likes as you? They probably like some of the same things as you, because friendships are often based on shared interests.

When you talk to new people, you can ask about things that they like and then relate to them. If you really like video games, you might talk about your favorite game and then ask the other person what kind of games they like.

TREAT OTHERS HOW YOU WANT TO BE TREATED

Do you remember back when you started school and you were told to always follow the Golden Rule? Treating other people the way you want to be treated is important. If you want someone to be a good friend to you, you need to start treating them like a good friend, too. Be kind to them. Try complimenting them on something about them or what they are doing. If you see someone wearing a backpack with your favorite video game character on it, you could always try saying you really like their backpack. This also gives you common ground with each other, which is a great way to get along and start making friends.

REMEMBER TO MAKE YOUR BODY LOOK FRIENDLY

When you go up to new people, how do you approach them? Do you approach them at all? If you hide in a corner behind your hair, or you don't look them in the eyes, they will think that you aren't interested in them, and they're probably not going to try talking to you. Would you want to talk to someone who stared at the ground? Probably not! You'd probably think they are ignoring you. The same goes for the people around you!

Friendly body language shows other people that you want to be talked to. This means it's important for you to smile. It's important for you to look other people in the eyes, especially when they are talking, so they know that you are paying attention. It's also usually a good idea to try talking as confidently as you can.

HAVE FUN!

One way to break the ice and get to know other people is to have some jokes. Try memorizing a few jokes so you can use them if you're ever stuck in a situation where you don't have anything to say to someone new.

TRY SOMETHING NEW

If you're having a hard time meeting new people, going out and trying something new can be a great way to find people that are interested in the same thing as you. Maybe you join a sports team or a club at school for people that share interests with you. Maybe you take music lessons. By going to new places and meeting new people, you find all sorts of new people who could become your friends.

ASK QUESTIONS

When you are talking to someone, it's a good idea to make sure they get a chance to talk, too. An easy way to start a conversation, which will go both ways, is to ask some questions about  the other person. Their answers can also tell you all about whether they share interests with you and can help you to better get along.

Chapter 8

HOW TO DO CHORES

Do you ever groan and moan when your grown-up tells you it's time to do chores? I get it! Chores aren't really fun for anyone, grown-ups included. Even though they're boring, it's still important to do them.

WHY SHOULD I DO CHORES? I'M NOT A GROWN-UP YET!

One day, you won't be a kid anymore. I know it seems a long way off now, but before you know it, you'll be all grown up, and you'll need to know how to take care of yourself. Chores can help you learn responsibility, and they also help you learn how to take care of yourself when you move away from your grown-ups into your own home.

The next time you want to ask your grown-up why you have to do chores when they're the grown-up and you're just a kid, remember some of these reasons that they are so important.

YOU LEARN THROUGH PRACTICE

Practice makes perfect, and when you're a kid, you've got lots of time to practice skills that you will need as a grown-up. You don't magically learn how to cook and clean when you turn 18! You have to take the time to learn those skills, and if your grown-ups are giving you chores, they're trying to help you learn them while you still have them there to help.

Yes, it might be boring to pick up all the dog toys and vacuum the floor or put away your laundry, but you need to learn how to take care of yourself. School will teach you lots of things you'll need to know, but it probably won't teach you how to wash the dishes or do the laundry.

YOU LEARN RESPONSIBILITY

When you have regular chores that you are expected to complete at home, you learn responsibility. Grown-ups need responsibility to be able to live by themselves. They have lots of things they have to juggle, like chores, work, and maybe even school and taking care of kids. It takes a lot of responsibility to be able to do all of it on time.

Instead of getting upset that your grown-ups want you to do chores around the house, take pride in knowing that you're learning the things you'll need as a grown-up. It shows how mature and big you are getting when you start doing your chores without being reminded.

YOU LEARN RESPECT

Do you know how much your grown-ups have to work for the things you have in your home? They spend a lot of time at work. Some may be at work so much, it feels like they live there instead of at home! When you don't take care of your home space, you show your grown-ups disrespect for all their hard work. You show them that you don't care about their time if you are making bigger messes for them to handle instead of cleaning up after yourself or doing the chores they assigned you.

YOU LEARN HOW TO WORK HARD

Working hard is called having a strong work ethic. This is an important skill that grown-ups need. A grown-up with a strong work ethic is able to do a lot of work on their own in a responsible way.

You will probably have to work a job like a grown-up at some point. Doing your chores without complaining and getting them on time now will help you develop a good work ethic that will help you later.

YOU HELP YOUR GROWN-UPS

Do your grown-ups ever get so tired, they fall asleep on the couch after a long day at work before bedtime? It takes a lot of work to be a grown-up, especially if you have kids! When you pitch in with the chores, whether because you were asked or because you wanted to do something nice, you show that you care about

your grown-ups and how they feel. Helping them out is a way to show how much you love and respect them, especially if you do something they didn't ask you to do.

KEEPING CHORES FUN

Chores might not be very fun on their own, but they can be if you turn them into a game! One way to make chores feel less boring is to turn them into games. It doesn't feel like work when you're having fun!

TURN YOUR CHORES INTO A GAME

Have you ever thought of turning your chores into a game? Maybe when you pick up all the dog toys, you have to race the clock to see how quickly you can do it, or you challenge one of your siblings to see who can pick up more before the job is done. There are lots of ways you can turn your chores into something more exciting.

PLAY FREEZE CLEAN

One fun way to do chores as a group is to put on some music and play Freeze Clean. It's just like Freeze Dance, only you're cleaning instead of dancing. Put one person in charge of the music, and when they freeze the music, everyone has to stop. Tally up points for whoever moves when the music is stopped, and at the end of the cleaning session, whoever has the least amount of points wins! Just make sure you take turns being in control of the music every 5 or 10 minutes!

GIVE A ROOM A MAKEOVER

Take pictures before you start cleaning a room, and then take pictures after. The goal is to make the room look like a brand new space, nice and clean.

BULLSEYE SWEEPING

Do you have to sweep? Make a goal or bullseye, using the dust pan or even some painter's tape, and try to sweep all of the dust to that one spot.

PLAY CHORE BINGO

Do you have a list of chores that you have to do? Make it a race with siblings or grown-ups by making a list of chores on a piece of paper. The first person to finish the list and mark off all their chores wins!

HELP YOUR GROWN-UP

Another way to make chores fun is to do them with a grown-up. There are lots of chores that you can help with that will teach you while you get the job done, and you get to spend some extra quality time with your grown-ups. Try cooking, folding laundry, or cleaning the floors together and see how you feel after.

Chapter 9

HOW TO HANDLE AN EMERGENCY

Do you know what to do if there's an emergency? Your first thought might be that that's what the grown-up needs to do, but sometimes, there are times when the kid needs to take action.

Emergencies can be scary, especially if you can't ask for help right away. You've probably already been taught to call 911 in an emergency if you really need the help, but do you know what to do in other cases?

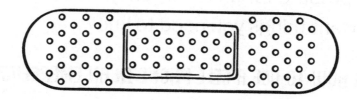

Learning to handle emergencies is an important life skill for everyone to know. We don't plan for emergencies to happen and we usually can't predict them, either. If we could, we'd be able to plan to make them not happen!

While you can't stop an emergency from happening on your own, you can prepare so you know what to do if one happens.

PREPARING FOR AN EMERGENCY

If an emergency happens, the best way to deal with it is to already be prepared. If you know what to expect and practice it with grown-ups, you know what to do if it ever happens. This is no different than practicing emergency drills at school. You practice when there's no danger so if there ever *is* danger, you will already know what to do and that will keep you calmer.

To prepare for an emergency, there are some important things you need to know.

LEARN HOW TO USE A CELL PHONE IN AN EMERGENCY

In many emergency situations, the first thing you will need to do is call for help. If you live in the United States, this is probably done by calling 911. When your parents were kids, they probably had house phones that anyone could use. Nowadays, people

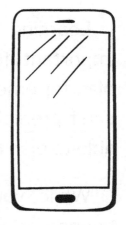

use cell phones instead, and your grown-ups probably have a lock on their screens.

Ask your grown-ups to show you how to use their phones in an emergency. Most phones have a button on the lock screen specifically for calling for help in an emergency. Talk about how to use it (but don't actually call it!) so if you ever need to, you can call for help.

LEARN IMPORTANT ADDRESSES AND PHONE NUMBERS

If you have to call for help, you will need to know your address and probably your grown-ups' phone numbers too. If you don't already have these memorized, now's a good time to learn it!

Did you know that you can memorize phone numbers by singing them to the tune of "Frere Jacques?" For example, if your phone number is (123) 456-7890, you would sing:

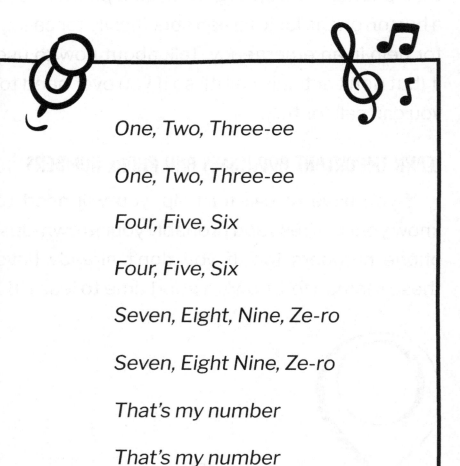

One, Two, Three-ee

One, Two, Three-ee

Four, Five, Six

Four, Five, Six

Seven, Eight, Nine, Ze-ro

Seven, Eight Nine, Ze-ro

That's my number

That's my number

You can learn your address using the same song. If your address were 567 Silly Street, Faketown, Oregon, you would sing:

Five, Six, Seven

Five, Six, Seven

Silly Street

Silly Street

Faketown, Oregon

Faketown, Oregon

That's my home

That's my home

LEARN FIRST AID

Do you know how to use a first aid kit? If you don't yet, it's a good idea to know how! In an emergency, it's possible that your grown-ups could get hurt and not be able to help you. Have a grown-up show you where your home keeps the first aid kit, and ask them to show you what's inside so you can learn how to use it.

Most first aid kits have bandages, wraps, ointments, and creams for wounds, and other important items that can help if someone gets hurt.

MAKING PLANS WITH GROWN-UPS

Every family should have an emergency plan that everyone knows so in an emergency, everyone can meet up again. The emergency plans that you need might look different than what they look like for another family, or someone who lives far away from you, because different areas have different natural emergencies. For example, if you live in California, you probably need an earthquake plan. If you live in Texas, you might need a hurricane and tornado plan, but you won't really need an earthquake plan.

No matter where you live, you should always have a plan for a fire.

CHOOSE MEETING SPOTS

The first step to setting up an emergency plan is choosing where you will meet your family if you get separated. You need two meeting spots. One should be close to your home, like in your front yard or across the street by the fire hydrant. Another should be a little bit further if it's not safe to stay close to your home, like down the block at a neighbor's home.

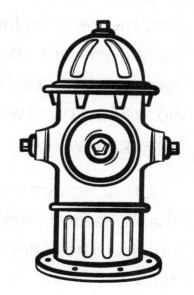

Make sure everyone knows where the meeting spots are so everyone goes to the right spot!

TALK ABOUT HOW TO GET OUT OF THE HOUSE

Sometimes, emergencies can make it difficult to get out of your home. A fire could block off the exit, or there could be something in your way keeping you from going through the door. Talk about other plans with  your grown-ups so you have other ways to get out. They probably already have plans for how to evacuate your home if you need to.

Some homes have more than one floor, and that means climbing out a window might not be easy if you are upstairs. Upstairs rooms should have emergency hanging ladders that can be hooked onto the window to climb out if in case of emergency.

Other homes may have fire escapes, or more than one door that you can go through to get outside. These are things to think about with your family.

TALK ABOUT SHELTERING IN THE HOME

Some emergencies mean that you have to stay in the home until the emergency passes, like tornadoes, earthquakes, and hurricanes. Do you have a plan with your family? Talk about the different ways you can shelter in place at home with your parents.

TORNADOES

In a tornado, the best place to shelter in place is in a ground-level or basement-level space with no windows. This might be a bathroom, hallway, or closet, depending on your home.

EARTHQUAKES

In an earthquake, it's important to get underneath a sturdy piece of furniture in case anything falls. Hide underneath a table, desk, or bed in whatever room or floor you are in until the earthquake stops. Never try to run up or down the stairs during an earthquake! You could fall or get hurt. Wait until the ground stops moving before trying to get to the rest of your family.

HURRICANES

Like a tornado, during a hurricane it's important to stay away from windows because the strong winds could make things break through the glass. Make sure that you follow your grown-ups' instructions while sheltering.

PRACTICE YOUR PLANS

Make sure that once you decide on how to deal with emergencies, you and your family practice sometimes so everyone remembers what to do if they ever need it. You should try to practice what to do during emergencies at least every six months to keep it fresh in your mind.

CALLING 911 IN AN EMERGENCY

Hopefully, this is a life skill you never have to use, but it's an important one to know. If you ever have to call for help during an emergency, you will probably call 911. It can be scary, especially because if you are calling, it's because your grown-ups can't do it themselves. These are the steps to calling for help in an emergency:

1. Remember your deep breathing skills! Use them and take a deep breath.

2. Call your local emergency number. For the United States, this is 911, but if you live somewhere else, make sure you ask your grown-ups what it is.

3. The person on the other line will ask you some questions. Answer them as best as you can. They will probably ask you what your emergency is, your name, and address, and then ask for details, like how many people need help and which emergency responders are needed. Be as detailed as possible! The more information you give the person on the phone, the more help you can get.

4. The operator on the phone will give you instructions on what to do before help arrives. Remember to follow what they say very carefully. Don't hang up until the operator says it's okay.

ROLEPLAYING EMERGENCY SITUATIONS

If you've made all your plans for what to do in an emergency, it's time to practice! Take the time with your grown-ups or siblings to practice these situations. You can even turn it into a roleplay game!

The more you practice, the more you will remember if an emergency ever happens. Here are a few scenarios to get you started.

SCENARIO 1

You're upstairs in your room when you hear a loud banging sound. When you go check it out, you see your grown-up on the ground. Your grown-up is bleeding and can't stand up or get to their phone. What do you do?

Answer: You call 911 and ask for help.

Roleplay the phone call with 911 with your grown-up or another family member. Don't forget to say what the emergency is, the address, and what you need help with.

SCENARIO 2

You're playing in your room when an earthquake starts! What do you do?

Answer: You hide underneath something heavy or get somewhere that nothing can fall on you and wait for the earthquake to stop.

SCENARIO 3

You wake up to your fire alarm beeping and smell smoke. Your bedroom door feels hot to the touch, so it's not safe to open it. How do you get out of the room?

Answer: This depends on your home's layout and family plan! Do what you discussed with your grown-ups to get out, and then meet them at the meeting spot.

Chapter 10

HOW TO HAVE A CHAMPION MINDSET

Do you have big goals in life? Do you want to do great things? A lot of kids do, and that's great! I believe that anyone can be anything they want, as long as they're willing to put in the work and they have a champion mindset.

A champion is someone who works hard to pursue their dreams. A champion knows how to focus to get past failure and gets where they want in life because they never give up. All of this can be summed up as having what we call a growth mindset.

Do you feel like you get discouraged easily? Do you have a hard time sticking to things that you start if you face a challenge? Try working on building a champion mindset for yourself.

HAVING A GROWTH MINDSET

When someone has a growth mindset, they believe that skills can be learned and grown. Do you think the best basketball players were born knowing how to throw the ball? No! They had to learn. That means that at one point, they were a beginner that had to learn everything, and they learned and practiced so much that they became one of the very best.

Even if something is hard for you right now, it's because you haven't learned how to do it yet. You haven't built up the skills to be an expert at whatever you try to do. If you think that you will never get better at something because you are bad at it now, that's called having a fixed mindset.

Fixed mindsets make it really hard to put in the effort to get better. It's easy to give up if you think you will never learn or grow. Having a growth mindset is the opposite.

TRY NEW THINGS

People with a growth mindset always push themselves to try new things. It's good to pursue the things you like to do, but it's also good to experience a variety of things. Learning new sports, games, and hobbies all help to grow your brain and teach you new skills that you might not have had before.

It's good for those new things to be challenging for you. If everything you do is easy, then you're not growing, are you? A growth mindset is all about learning and growing. Champions never stop learning or trying to improve, and neither should you!

BE PERSISTENT

When you're feeling frustrated, you might feel like you want to give up and quit. If you do, you never really improve, which isn't good for you either. Persistence is learning to keep trying, even when it's hard and even if you fail the first, second, or even tenth try. The more you practice and try, the closer you'll get to succeeding, and one day, you'll do it!

The next time you feel like giving up, stop and think about why you want to quit. Will quitting something make you feel any better, or will it just make you feel bad for giving up? If you play a sport with a team, will you feel good if you quit and leave your team short one person? Is that really better than having you, even if you're not as good at it as you want to be?

CHANGE HOW YOU THINK ABOUT WINNING AND LOSING

Winning and losing aren't the most important things in a growth mindset. Sure, it's nice to win, and it's no fun to lose, but both give you ideas on how to keep growing. If you win because you really put a lot of effort into something, then congratulations! That's exactly what you're supposed to do with a growth mindset. You keep trying and the effort pays off. If you won without much effort, on the other hand, it's not really a good thing. It says that you're not pushing yourself to keep growing and learning.

Losing isn't a bad thing either. When you lose, you might feel disappointed, especially if you put a lot of effort into it, but losing just means that you have room to improve! It means that you have something to keep working toward, and your effort will pay off! There's no reason to quit. If the only reason you are doing something is to win or lose, you might want to think about whether the activity is important to you, or if winning is. As you continue to practice and grow in certain activities, the important part is having fun and growing as a person.

CHANGE HOW YOU THINK ABOUT CONSTRUCTIVE CRITICISM

When you work toward something, no matter what it is, you'll probably hear constructive criticism. To criticize something is to say what is wrong with it. When someone gives you constructive criticism, they are giving you information about where you could improve in a way that is meant to help you.

Constructive criticism can sound an awful lot like criticism at first, especially if it comes right after you messed something up. Instead of getting upset or bothered by what is said, what if you looked at it as help?

You can also give yourself constructive criticism if you know what the right questions to ask are. Try asking yourself if things went according to your plans, and if they didn't, ask yourself what you would do differently in the future.

Constructive criticism will happen sometimes. If you use it to help yourself improve, you are developing a growth mindset and are one step closer to having that champion mindset that will help you to succeed.

Chapter 11

HOW TO SET A ROUTINE YOU CAN STICK TO

Routines might seem boring, but they're really good tools for keeping yourself on track. Think about what you do every day. You probably wake up, get ready for school, have breakfast, go to school all day, then come home and do homework for a little while. Then, you get ready for bed and do it all over again.

Is it boring? Sometimes, yes.

Is it important? Yes, absolutely!

A routine is good for your body because it learns what to expect. That's why you always get hungry right around the time you eat lunch at school, or why you're sleepy at the same time at night.

Learning how to set a routine you can stick to helps you to get all of the things you need to get done each day and gives you more time to do what you want to.

Your routine will probably include a time to wake up and go to school, a time to come home to do homework and chores, time to spend on activities and fun, and time to get ready for bed.

WHY ARE ROUTINES HARD?

Routines feel hard for kids because usually, you don't get very much control over it. Your grown-ups probably set the routine for you and expect you to follow it. This can be helpful in making sure everything gets done, but what if it doesn't work for you?

It's easy to get distracted, feel overwhelmed, or struggle to keep track of time. To follow your routine, you need to be able to do all of these things:

- Keep track of all of your time

- Change tasks when you are supposed to

- Remember all the steps of all the things you need to do

- Not get distracted

- Follow the rules

- Organize and plan everything you need to do

This can be hard for kids because your brains are still developing. These skills are called executive functioning skills, and the part of your brain that controls it doesn't finish developing until you're already a grown-up! This means that even if you really, really, *really* want to stick to your routine, it's going to be harder for you than it is for someone older than you. That's why it's important to learn how to make a routine that you can stick to, and learn some tricks to help you focus.

MAKING A ROUTINE

Making a routine is the easiest part. All you have to do is make yourself a schedule. If you can, talk to your grown-ups about setting up a routine and creating a daily schedule that you can put on your bedroom wall or on the fridge so you can look at it if you ever need help remembering what you're supposed to be doing.

WRITE DOWN EVERYTHING YOU NEED TO DO EACH DAY

To start, write down all your daily tasks that you need to do on notecards or sticky notes and write down how long it takes underneath them. You'll be organizing them later, so you want to be able to move things nice and easily. Some common things that you will need to do in a day include:

- Breakfast, lunch, and dinner

- Brushing teeth and showering

- School

- Homework

- Chores (list these out!)

- Activities and sports

- Things you do on a schedule with your family

ORGANIZE YOUR LIST

Once you have a pile of notecards or sticky notes of all your daily activities, you can start sorting them. I like to sort them into morning, day, and nighttime activities. Move things that need to be done in the morning into the morning pile, and repeat this for the daytime and nighttime piles.

MAKE A DAILY TIMELINE

When you have an idea of what you need to do in the morning, daytime, and nighttime, you can start putting the activities in order. If you wrote down how long each activity will take you, you should have a good idea of what time things need to happen to make sure everything gets done. Set up an order to what you need to do that makes sense, and then start putting times to each one.

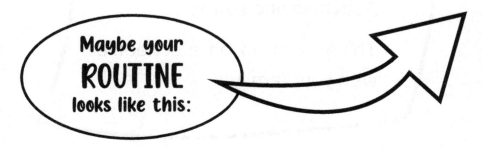

Maybe your
ROUTINE
looks like this:

7:00 AM: Wake up

7:05 AM: Brush teeth, use the toilet, and get dressed

7:20 AM: Eat breakfast

7:40 AM: Pack backpack and put on shoes

7:50 AM: Go to school

2:45 PM: Come home from school. Snack and free time until 3:30!

3:30 PM: Homework

4:30 PM: Start chores

4:30 PM: Let dogs out

4:40 PM: Pick up bedroom

5:00 PM: Put away any toys or school stuff in common areas

5:20 PM: Take trash out of bedroom and bathroom

5:30 PM: Karate

7:00 PM: Dinner

7:30 PM: Finish homework

8:30 PM: Free time

9:30 PM: Shower, brush teeth, and get ready for bed

9:45 PM: Reading time

10:15 PM: Bedtime

TRY TO STICK TO IT

Once you have your schedule, it's time to stick to it. One of the easiest ways to stick to it is to set up reminders. Does your family have an Amazon Echo? Alexa can remind you to do things throughout the day to help you remember what you need to do. If you don't, you can also use a tablet or phone to set up the reminders for you.

Just remember that when your reminder goes off, it's important to do what you are supposed to do right away, if you can. It's not good to put things off, because if you do, you'll mess up your schedule for the rest of the day.

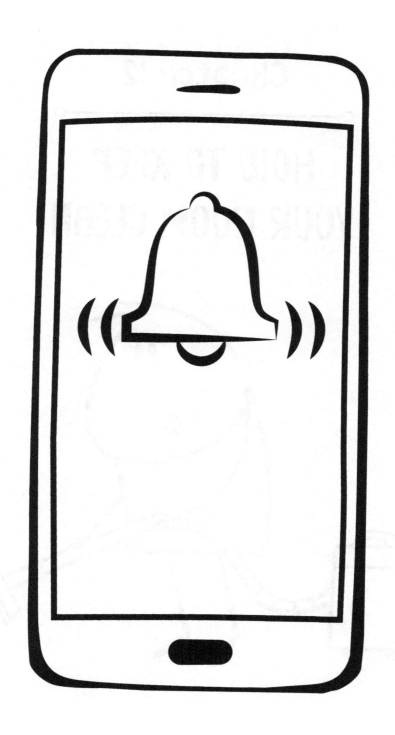

Chapter 12

HOW TO KEEP YOUR ROOM CLEAN

When you walk into your bedroom, is it clean or a big mess? A messy room can make it hard to focus or find the things you need. If your space is a mess, you'll probably have a hard time finding the things you need when doing homework and other activities.

Keeping a room clean can seem like a big pain, but if you add keeping it clean to your routine and do a few little things each day, you can do it!

WHY SHOULD I WANT A CLEAN BEDROOM?

A clean bedroom is important for lots of reasons. First, it means that your room is safer. Remember how we talked about what to do in an emergency? If there's ever an emergency or a fire where you have to get out of your room quickly, a mess will make this harder. You need to be able to get to doors and windows safely.

Keeping a clean room also will teach you how to take care of your things. If you leave your toys and books wherever they fall, they'll probably get stepped on and broken. If you have a dog, your dog might think the things on the floor are toys and eat them. Right now, your grown-ups probably pay for everything you have, but when you are all grown, you have to pay for everything. Learning to take care of your things now will help you when you are older.

Your clean room also becomes your own safe space. It's somewhere comfy you can go when you need some time to yourself. You can be proud of your clean room.

HOW CAN I CLEAN MY ROOM WHEN IT'S A BIG MESS?

When your room is a big mess, it can be overwhelming to know what to do first. A big mess can feel impossible to clean, but there are ways to make it easier.

BREAK IT DOWN

If your room is a mess, there are probably a whole lot of things you need to do. You probably need to pick up dirty clothes, put away toys, clean up clutter, and do a bunch of other things. Instead of looking at it as one big mess, try seeing it as lots of little messes. This will make it easier to manage.

MAKE A LIST OF TASKS

Write down a list of everything you need to do in your room before you get started and after you break down the mess. Maybe your list looks like this:

- Pick up dirty clothes
- Put away stuffed animals
- Put away blocks
- Put away arts and crafts
- Put away other toys
- Make bed
- Throw away trash
- Put away books
- Clean desk
- Clean closet

That looks like a lot of stuff, but most of those jobs will only take you a few minutes at a time to finish.

WORK ON ONE TASK AT A TIME

Start working on your list of things to do. Try focusing on one task at a time. Then, every time you finish a task, you can cross it off your list and celebrate a little bit. Be proud of yourself for finishing it! Take a minute or two to cheer, and then move on to the next one.

When you finish one task, the good feelings you get can motivate you to work on the next one, too.

TAKE BREAKS BETWEEN TASKS

If you have a really big mess that's going to take longer than 30 minutes to finish, take breaks every now and then. After three little tasks or one or two big tasks, give yourself five or ten minutes as a break before getting back to work. Little breaks can really help you from feeling overwhelmed.

MAKE IT FUN!

Do you like cleaning in a quiet room? I know I don't. Putting music on while you clean gives you something to listen to while you get your work done. Plus, some fun, upbeat music can really raise your mood while you do something you don't like to do and help the time pass by quicker.

KEEP GOING UNTIL IT'S DONE

The last thing for you to do is to keep working until you're done! Before you know it, you'll have a nice, clean room, and then all you'll need to do is keep it clean.

HOW CAN I KEEP MY ROOM CLEAN?

Keeping your room clean is pretty easy, but it does mean that you have to clean a little bit every day. You can't just clean your room and leave it because as you use it, it'll just become a big mess again. Little cleans every day will keep the big mess from coming, even though you'll have to do it more often. You'll have less work when you do have to clean. This means you can spend more time doing what you want!

To keep your room clean, you need to learn some new habits. They might be hard at first. Habits take a long time to build, but once they're there, it's easy to keep up with them.

PUT THINGS AWAY WHEN YOU'RE DONE WITH THEM

The first way to help you keep your room clean is to put things you use away as soon as you're finished. If you take off some dirty clothes, put them right in your dirty laundry bin. If you get a load of clean laundry from your grown-ups, put them away right away.

Whenever you finish playing with a toy or reading a book or making a craft, put everything away. It only takes a minute or two to clean up the little mess, but it'll take much, much longer if you let everything build up.

Make it a habit to put something away as soon as you no longer need it.

CLEAN UP MESSES THAT TAKE LESS THAN FIVE MINUTES

If you notice that you have a little mess somewhere, like if something gets knocked down and spills, picking it up right away helps keep the mess from building up, too. If a mess will take you less than five minutes to clean, do it as soon as you notice it needs to get done. The five minutes won't make much of a difference to your day unless you're really in a rush, but it will make a difference when it keeps your room clean.

MAKE YOUR BED EACH MORNING

Making your bed in the morning is an important habit that can benefit you in many ways! First, it can give you a sense of accomplishment and help you start your day off on the right foot. Plus, it can make your room look neater and more organized, which can help you feel more relaxed and less stressed. By taking a few minutes to straighten your sheets and fluff your pillows, you can create a cozy and inviting space that you'll be excited to come back to at the end of the day. So why not give it a try? You might be surprised at how much of a difference it can make!

SPEND 10 MINUTES CLEANING YOUR ROOM EACH DAY BEFORE YOU HAVE FUN

It can be tempting to run off and play when there are things to be done, but if you do your work first, you'll have more time to play later. Take ten minutes each day to clean up your space before you go have fun. Then, you know your work is done for the day and all you have to do is put things away as soon as you're done with them.

HAVE A PLACE FOR EVERYTHING

Everything in your room should have a place where it goes. If something doesn't have a place, choose one for it. If you can't find a place for something, it's time to think about whether you need to have it in your room at all.

To get organized, think of good places for things to go. Your clothes are probably organized into drawers or hanging in a closet. Books should  go on a shelf or in a bin. Toys should have bins to keep them organized. Your desk shouldn't be a big explosion of arts and crafts and should be organized.

You might need to ask for help from a grown-up to find good places for your things, but once you choose a place, stick with it!

Chapter 13

HOW TO COOK SAFELY

Everyone should learn how to cook. You need to know how to take care of yourself and part of that is learning how to cook. As a kid, it's not safe for you to cook without permission or a grown-up watching you.

At eight years old, you are old enough to start learning how to cook easy foods with a grown-up. This might look like helping your grown-up when they make dinner, or it could be making yourself food during the day.

Before you run to the kitchen and pull out all the pans, there are some things you'll need to know first.

KITCHEN SAFETY RULES

In the kitchen, there are a lot of dangerous things. Knives, a hot pan, and even raw meats and ingredients can be dangerous. You probably don't know all the rules yet, but you can start learning them now.

KEEP YOUR HANDS CLEAN

It's important to keep your hands clean when you cook or make food. Think about all the things you touch during the day. You might pick up garbage to throw away, or pet your dog, or touch the floor while playing. All of these things are covered in germs that get onto your hands.

If you don't wash your hands often and then touch your food, you put germs on your food that can make you sick when you eat them. You should always wash your hands before touching food and when eating. You should also always wash your hands whenever you touch ingredients that could have germs, like raw meat or eggs.

Remember to scrub your hands for at least 30 seconds with soap and hot water to wash away all the germs.

CLEAN WHILE YOU COOK

Just like you should clean as you go about your day in your room, you should clean while you cook. It's easier to throw away a wrapper or scraps of food a little at a time as you make them than it is to make a big, messy pile that has to all be cleaned up.

Messes can be dangerous in kitchens, too. If you spill water on the floor, you could slip while cooking and that's not safe for anyone.

LISTEN TO INSTRUCTIONS

When cooking with a grown-up, listen carefully to their instructions and follow them. Those instructions are given to you to keep you safe and teach you the right way to cook.

BE CAREFUL WITH KNIVES AND HOT FOOD

Knives, hot foods and pans, and the oven and stove can be dangerous if you're not careful. It is very easy to burn or cut yourself in the kitchen, and that's why you should listen to your grown-up when they give you instructions.

Practice good knife skills with your grown-ups with knives that can't cut you at first, and as you get better, you can start using sharper ones.

Don't ever grab a hot pan without a potholder and be careful when handling hot foods so you don't get hurt. Ask your grown-up to show you the right way to hold or carry a pot of hot food.

If you feel like you can't do something safely in the kitchen, don't forget to ask for help! It's always better to ask for help to do something safely than to try to do something potentially dangerous all by yourself.

FOLLOW A RECIPE

Following a recipe is a good way to learn how to cook new foods. Your grown-ups probably followed recipes when learning how to cook, and probably still do now, even if you don't see it. If you find a recipe that you want to make, this is the easiest way to follow it.

READ THE INSTRUCTIONS BEFORE YOU BEGIN

Make sure you read all of the instructions before you get started. Some people like to do it at least twice before moving on. When you read, make sure you have all of the ingredients and that you can do all of the steps.

PREPARE AND MEASURE ALL OF THE INGREDIENTS BEFORE YOU BEGIN

Before you start cooking, it's always best to get all of the ingredients ready. This is when you chop up things that need to be chopped, measure out salt, milk, and other ingredients, and beat your eggs. It might seem like it will take you longer if you measure all of your ingredients before you start cooking, but this will make it faster and you can clean up the mess as you go.

FOLLOW THE DIRECTIONS STEP BY STEP

Once all your ingredients are prepped and ready, you can start cooking! Follow the steps the way they are written and ask for help if you need it.

Even if your recipe doesn't come out quite right the first time, that's okay! You're still learning. Just keep working at it and before you know it, you'll be a pro cook in no time.

CONCLUSION

Every day is an opportunity to learn something new. It's an opportunity to develop your skills and get better at what you do. Even if something doesn't quite go how you planned it, it's important to remember that you are still learning!

At your age, you still have a long time until you will be a grown-up. That's a lot of time for you to work on those life skills that you will need when you are older. Remember, having a champion mindset is all about remembering to keep working on things even when they get hard. It's remembering to take every experience as a way to learn, even if things don't work out the first time.

These skills give you a foundation. When you build a house, you need a foundation to hold up all the rest of it. Skills are the same way. You learn foundations and build up on top of them to learn more and more. The skills in this book help you to learn more skills that you will need as you keep growing up. You can do it!

LEAVE YOUR FEEDBACK ON AMAZON

Please think about leaving some feedback via a review on Amazon. It may only take a moment, but it really does mean the world for small authors like myself :)

Even if you did not enjoy this title, please let me know the reason(s) in your review so that I may improve this title and serve you better.

FROM THE AUTHOR

As a retired school teacher, my mission with this series is to create premium educational content for children that will help them be strong in the body, mind, and spirit via important life lessons and skills.

Without you, however, this would not be possible, so I sincerely thank you for your purchase and for supporting my life's mission.

DON'T FORGET YOUR
FREE GIFTS!

(My way of saying thank you for your support)

Simply visit
haydenfoxmedia.com
to receive the following:

10 Powerful Dinner Conversations
To Create Amazing Kids

10 Magnificent Affirmations
To Help Kids Become Unstoppable In Life

(You can also scan this QR code)

More titles
you're sure to love!

HAYDEN FOX

Made in the USA
Middletown, DE
07 September 2024

60581090R00076